What others are saying about this book:

"I went out with a 'new guy' who was nice and Extremely Attractive. But with my life partner list still fresh in my mind, I realized even though he had striking features, he was a no-go for me. The life partner list made the difference and saved me from another big time-waster."
Jeanine H.

"My love life is finally working for me and I'm having a ball! You have unleashed a tiger."
Joanne P.

"I don't know if I'd have recognized Michael if it wasn't for my list. I can't tell you how happy I am. There's nothing better than being in love with a very good man and having so much in common."
Laura W.

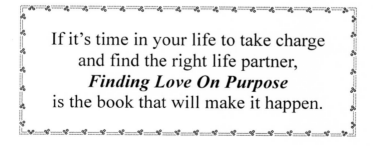

If it's time in your life to take charge
and find the right life partner,
Finding Love On Purpose
is the book that will make it happen.

finding
love
on purpose

with the
Life Partner

Earl Hipp

Human Resource Development, Inc.
Minneapolis, MN

Published by:
Human Resource Development, Inc.
2938 Monterey Ave.
Minneapolis, MN 55416

Website: http://www.FindingLoveOnPurpose.com

For permission to quote this book contact the publisher at:
Publisher@HRD-Inc.com

International Standard Book Number (ISBN): 0-9741324-1-1
Library of Congress Control Number: 2004105392

Cover art designed by Bret Slattengren
Cover design by Manoj Vijayan at Marketing Edge Design

Table of Contents

Table of Contents

Acknowledgments

If you ever walk this path, you'll understand why authors feel so humble and why they always include an Acknowledgements page to honor the people who helped make the book possible. So to give my helpers a tiny bit of the praise they deserve, I hereby honor and thank:

The dozen or so single friends who made up the pilot *Finding Love On Purpose* team.

Cynthia Harris, my friend and long-standing editorial ally. My editorial team also includes Linda Tucker, Larry Wurst and Elizabeth Ohm.

My trendy nephew Bret Slattengren for the cover design.

Eva Almeida, for her invaluable support and for her very helpful website: http://www.booksnbytes.com

Matt Cohen, my unwavering Web Guy.

Greg Loumeau at Dreamco Media for help with the book design and for his supportive and encouraging inputs.

My sweet life partner Gwen, for her understanding, support, and objectivity on this project. It's not easy living with a writer.

You! Thank you for caring enough about yourself and this important part of your life to buy this book and for your commitment to finding love on purpose.

From the Author

Finding Love On Purpose has been written for people who are ready to do what's necessary to find the *right* life partner. Choosing a life partner is one of the most important decisions we ever make, yet we are given little, if any, direct training in how to go about finding that person. As a result, too many people make their life partner decisions based on random encounters, other people's suggestions, romantic ideals, or the chemistry of the moment. In doing so, they are leaving way too much to chance.

The most important step in finding love on purpose is to get a clear, even precise, understanding about what attributes you want in a life partner. When you know *exactly* who you're looking for, you're better prepared to recognize a solid prospect and can avoid wasting time and emotional energy on people who aren't "it." The truly wonderful benefit of clarity about your life partner is when you meet someone who fits your criteria, you can safely enter the romantic dance with your heart fully open.

My motivation to help you find the right life partner comes from my background as a therapist, my own life partner quest, and more than ten years of coaching people. Over that period, I've evolved a proven process that will help you find love, on purpose. Doing this work is the very best way to take charge of your relationship life. It's doing what you can, on purpose, to be able to recognize and connect with the love of your life.

My wish for you is that you'll find the wonderful partner you want and deserve. It's the reason I wrote this book and why it's in your hands now. I commend you for taking control of this key part of your life, and I wish you success beyond your dreams.

Earl Hipp
Minneapolis, Minnesota

About the Author

Earl Hipp is an author and professional speaker. He and his life partner, Gwen, live in Minneapolis, Minnesota, in the summer, and Tucson, Arizona, in the winter. He enjoys spending time with his family and friends, hiking in the mountains, playing at the ocean, traveling to beautiful places, a good cup of coffee, and just being quiet.

Earl always enjoys hearing from his readers. Send him your stories about finding love on purpose, any questions you have about this process, or ideas for another book. You can e-mail him directly at:

Author@FindingLoveOnPurpose.com

Dedication
To people with broken hearts
who have lost hope.

To people with the courage
to dream.

Introduction

You're reading this because you are attracted to the idea of finding your best possible life partner. I'm going to assume at least some of the following statements are also more or less true:

- You have spent considerable time, emotional energy, and money trying to meet the "right" person to become your life partner.

- You've been in a few relationships and have learned some important lessons about the qualities in a partner that work for you and those that don't. You have turned those lessons into a vague notion of what you want and don't want in a life partner candidate.

- You've put aside the painful losses of previous relationships and are willing to continue to search for a high-quality life partner in spite of your fear of another "failure."

- You're holding on to the hope the right person is out there, that you can find him or her, and the two of you will have a wonderful and satisfying life together.

If this sounds at all like you, *Finding Love On Purpose* will put you in charge and provide the necessary guidance to help you find your best possible life partner.

The process described in this book has led me to my own wonderful life partner, and it has connected many couples who are now married or in other forms of committed relationships. It has even gotten my shy, eighty-year-old, opera-loving neighbor Bill, twelve dates. As you'll soon discover, this approach always works if you're willing to invest your time and energy.

Your story might be similar to that of my friend Aimee. She was 26 years old, established in her career, and ready to make finding a life partner a priority. "All my friends were married and starting families and I was feeling a little behind schedule," Aimee admitted. She'd go to bars with her crew of pals from school, and friends occasionally fixed her up. But none of these fellows panned out. After one big relationship disappointment, she slipped into despair.

After some time had passed, I suggested to Aimee that she begin anew and revitalize herself by making her first life partner list (which you'll see a little later). Once started, her list making activities brought optimism and confidence rushing back. Less than a year later, Aimee and her new husband heard their best man read her life partner list out loud at their wedding dinner. He was using it to publicly determine whether her new husband was qualified for the job!

The approach to finding love on purpose described in this book is a guided, five-step process for creating and refining a life partner list. At its simplest, the list is a description of attributes which paint a picture of your best possible life partner. As the list is developed, it becomes a compelling vision of your life together. Because your life partner list comes out of your life experiences and self-understanding, once completed, it will give you a very clear goal, and powerful motivational energy. In the *Finding Love On Purpose* process you will learn:

- Why people without a life partner list can only wander through relationships, relying on luck, and endlessly repeat the "Random Relationship Cycle."

- That for better or worse you already have a life partner list guiding your relationship choices. It's a list you didn't consciously create and which is too vague to provide reliable guidance.

- How a consciously created and refined life partner list allows you to identify, locate, and connect with great prospects.

- The absolute best times to create your life partner list.

- Five simple steps for creating, refining, and prioritizing a great life partner list.

- Seven proven strategies for taking your life partner list into the world and finding love on purpose. Including how you can successfully use your list with online and other matchmaking services.

- How to use your life partner list as a guide to help you decide how much time and emotional energy to invest in a prospect, and to help you avoid repeating dead-end relationships.

- How to recognize your prospective life partner when he or she shows up, and how to make sure the person has enough "right" for you to confidently step onto the path toward full commitment.

I know you're excited about getting started, but first you'll need just a little background on why doing this work is necessary and how the process actually works to help you meet the right person. Let's start by considering why you need a life partner list at all.

Why You Need a Life Partner List

There are at least two compelling reasons for creating a great life partner list:

> **The first** reason is that whether you realize it or not, you have always had an unconscious list that has been shaping your relationship choices. Given that fact, why not have a great list, which you've created intentionally, and fits the person you are today?

> **The second reason**, as strange as it may sound, is that having a well-thought-out list is the absolute best way to open your heart to romance when the "right" person comes along.

Habitual Patterns of Attraction

Have you noticed that the same type of people keep showing up in your life as partner material? This isn't so much a reflection of "what's out there," but a response to how your internal search engine is programmed.

The people you're unconsciously attracted to, the people who catch your eye when you look at a crowded room, and those who are drawn to you in response to your "signals," are all a reflection of your unconscious list which, for better or worse, determines *who* you see. You'll learn more about this amazing concept in the "How the List Works" section.

Jim is a man who suddenly became aware of his unconscious list working in his life. "During the early years following my divorce," he said, "I would frequent lots of singles events and dances where, without my knowing it, my unconscious list was operating very well. I wasn't aware until a friend of mine pointed out how often he was drawn to a woman across the dance floor, only to discover after chatting with her for a while, she'd always be very much like his ex-wife. This bit of information made me realize I was doing the same thing and got me thinking about my own habitual patterns of attraction."

If the wrong people keep showing up in your life, you may want to look at your "habitual patterns of attraction." If you don't go after love on purpose, by intentionally creating and then using a positive and relevant life partner list, your unconscious list will continue to function in background. Like a powerful relationship auto-pilot, it will subtly influence your choices and insure you get the same results . . . over and over again.

Your Unconscious Life Partner List
Some of the ways your unconscious life partner list has evolved may include:

- Your parents' role modeling. No matter what kind of parents you had, they taught you powerful lessons about what being in a relationship would/should/could be like. Who they were (even if they weren't present) and how they related to each other helped define the template for your original life partner list. Their relationship is your core model, even though you've unconsciously added many other elements over the years.

- Powerful expectations about your ideal partner, held by your parents or other family members, which were communicated to you in subtle or not-so-subtle ways.

- The relationship partners and styles you've seen in the movies, on television programs, and in advertising that have "taught" you what's desirable and what you should expect.

- The mountains of advice about partner selection you have absorbed from books and magazines.

- Your desire to clone the mates of your friends who appear happy in their relationships.

- The attributes your friends seem to think are important, based on the type of people they keep trying to fix you up with, and who they think would be "just perfect" for you.

Many of these influences are powerfully influencing your life partner search engine right now. Few of these factors have anything to do with the person you are today, and as a result, your unconscious list can't possibly point you to your best life partner.

The bottom line: If you don't intentionally, and in detail, re-program yourself with a current and relevant life partner list, you will continue to meet the people you are unconsciously programmed to find. Your habitual patterns of attraction will very predictably lead you to people who might be interesting or even exciting, but probably not good long-term candidates. As you go through the steps ahead, remember, some kind of list is always operating. Making a great list now is really the only way to take control of your relationship life and find love on purpose.

The first reason for making your life partner list is to be able to make informed and conscious choices about your prospective life partner. In the next section you will learn about the second reason for making a good life partner list . . . it just happens to be the best, and maybe only, way to open your heart to romance when the "right" person comes along.

Using Your Head to Open Your Heart

People who have been in and out of relationships a time or two are often living with resentments, damaged self-esteem, as well as some degree of fear about the next relationship. In a world where the divorce rate is hovering around sixty percent, you have a lot of people who are in a defensive, self-protecting posture when it comes to the next person who comes along.

The second reason for making a solid life partner list is that if you are certain a candidate is the "right" person, it will be easier to let down your guard and be open to the sweetness and romance of moving toward a new relationship.

> *This kind of certainty comes but once in a lifetime.*
> —Clint Eastwood, *Bridges of Madison County*

Without a clear and relevant life partner list, your search can only be random, based on chance connections and driven by your habitual patterns of attraction. Instead of actually finding love on purpose, people move into relationships because they are

- living with the loneliness of being single
- feeling tactile or sexual hungers
- being socially cut off because most of their friends are in relationships
- experiencing the fear of getting older . . . alone
- missing the structure, comforts, and routines of being in a relationship

Because of the power of these drives, it's easy to be confused about your feelings. It's very tempting to want to be in just *any* relationship instead of intentionally going for the solid connection that can form the basis of a successful long-term relationship.

Being in the wrong relationship for the wrong reasons may be interesting, dramatic, passionate, and may satisfy some of your short-term needs. But in the end, another relationship that isn't "it" only adds another painful life experience. It can also increase your hopelessness and defensiveness going into the next round.

> *I wonder how many more times*
> *I'm gonna fall for the same kind of cowboy?*
> —Belle Floyd, 1900, Cowgirlsgame.com

The Random Relationship Cycle

Because most people are on random access with their life partner search, disappointment, confusion, hopelessness, and an eventual closed heart are almost guaranteed. If you've been in a number of relationships, you may have noticed a predictable, circular, and self-esteem-destroying cycle of events taking place. A condensed version of this cycle looks something like this:

The Random Relationship Cycle

You feel the hunger for all the joys and comforts a good relationship can provide and (again) decide it's time to find the person of your dreams.

You head off in search of a great life partner with your vague or unconscious list operating in the background. You predictably make the same kinds of choices.

After the rush of blind love, excitement, and passion subsides, reality sets in. The relationship gradually begins to disintegrate because the person who looked so good initially isn't really "the one."

Weeks, months or many years later, in the ending phase of the relationship, one or both of you get hurt. After it ends, you retreat into the safety of social isolation where the feelings of anger, self-doubt, loneliness, and hopelessness thrive.

After a while, powerful relationship hungers begin to build again, and you decide you must do something.

With the memory of past relationship "failures" lurking, you tentatively decide to go for it again. This time you try to be more careful and not make the same choices, but because nothing has really changed and you're using the same unconscious life partner list, you instinctively pick the same type of person.

The cycle repeats itself… endlessly.

This is like deja vu all over again.
—Yogi Berra

Laura is making her life partner list to avoid another dead-end relationship. She describes the haphazard approach to finding a partner she's observed in so many others. "I've known a lot of desperate people looking for love. For some, it had been a long time since they had intimate physical or emotional contact, and others had experienced many relationships that didn't have enough right. But in every case, they were fearful, desperate, and lonely. I think most single people fall into this category to some degree. Perhaps this acting blindly out of desperation explains why people make so many bad choices and the same kinds of relationships are repeated so often."

Although relationships never come with guarantees, the best way to feel safe, optimistic, and have an open heart in the life partner search is to recalibrate your search engine so you'll know when the "right" person shows up.

When you're sure a new person has many of the attributes you have consciously decided are important, you'll feel more comfortable letting down your guard and opening your heart to the sweetness and romance of moving toward that person without fear.

When you set out to
find love on purpose,
you lead with your head
so you can open your heart.
—Earl Hipp

Immature love says:
I love you because I need you.
Mature love says:
I need you because I love you.
—Erich Fromm

How the List Works

A consciously created and refined life partner list changes everything. It not only becomes an invaluable guide as you set out to find love on purpose, but it changes you. As you will soon learn, working through the five steps of this process will greatly increase your clarity, make you more intentional, boost your optimism, and actually alter your vision in a way that makes good prospects easier to see.

Getting Clear and Intentional

Most people approach the search for the right partner like going to the grocery store without a shopping list when they're hungry. In that condition, you are more likely to spend time wandering the aisles, hoping to find something to make you feel better. Typically, you come away with food you purchased on impulse, much of which isn't good for you. On the other hand, if you make your grocery list when you're not hungry, you can be very clear about what you need. Then when you go to the store you can go directly to the items you want, avoid the impulse items, get what's good for you, and check out more quickly.

When you reprogram your relationship search engine with a well-thought-out shopping list, you have a solid tool to filter relationship candidates. You'll have a comforting anchor in reason and enough confidence in your choices to make stepping into a relationship, or walking away from the wrong person, less confusing.

Having clarity about the attributes of a great life partner, based on your life experience and the objectivity of a few trusted allies, makes the search for your partner more efficient, rational, safe, and ultimately much more romantic.

> *I think men who have a pierced ear*
> *are better prepared for marriage.*
> *They've experienced pain and bought jewelry.*
> —Rita Rudner

Managing Your Emotional Investment

Because of your list, when a prospective life partner shows up, you'll quickly get a sense of whether or not to proceed. Still, many of the attributes you want in a partner are subtle and won't be apparent immediately. As you continue to get to know the person, your list will help you decide, at each step, if you should continue to develop the relationship.

When you realize a person isn't "the one" based on your list, you may continue to see him or her because it's fun, you have something to learn, or you have common interests that could form the basis of a friendship. In this situation, the information from your life partner list will help you to intentionally manage the amount of time and emotional energy you invest.

Anne described how she put her list to work immediately after its creation. "I had been working on my list on Saturday, and on Sunday I went out with a 'new guy.' He was attractive and very nice, but with the list fresh in my mind, I found myself checking him out in a new way. As the evening rolled along, I realized that even though he was a good man with some striking features, he was a no-go for me. The list came through and I'm very grateful."

Being intentional, clear, and confident feels great in the life partner quest. But it gets even better. Keep reading to learn how list making dramatically changes how you see the world.

The Power of Selective Perception

The French novelist Marcel Proust said in the early 1900s, "The real journey of discovery is not in seeing new landscapes, but in having new eyes." Proust didn't know it, but he was describing the psychological phenomenon known as selective perception.

As we go through our daily lives, we're assaulted with a vast amount of information. To protect us from overload, our wonderful human brain automatically, unconsciously, and selectively sorts out the information that has value to us. Everything else becomes background noise. Selective perception is the primary skill you'll use to find love on purpose . . . after you've created your life partner list.

I drive a Subaru. It's actually a six-cylinder, white, LL Bean-edition, Subaru Outback wagon. Thanks to selective perception, out of the hundred thousand or so cars I pass every day, I'm able to quickly and easily pick out other white Subaru Outback wagons, instantly determine if they are the six-cylinder, LL Bean edition, and if so, smile and wave at the drivers. I notice these cars because I've programmed myself with very specific Subaru information. Chances are you notice a car "just like yours" when you pass it on the road. In addition to the car you drive, this skill works well for "cars with flashing red lights on the roof." Without selective perception, all you'd see when you're driving in traffic are "cars."

Just as in adjusting the lens on a camera, making a great life partner list sharpens your focus and changes what and who you see. That's why, like Proust, I'm suggesting you get "new eyes" for your "journey of discovery." It's entirely possible that every day as you go about your life, you're passing right by your ideal life partner. Until you get clear about the details of what you're looking for, he or she could be standing right in front of you and all you'd see are "people."

Selective perception not only helps you sort through all the distractions but helps you to react differently to what you see. You can be sure I have a very different response to white Subaru Outback wagons than I do to cars with flashing red lights on top.

When it comes to finding love on purpose,
what you get is very much
what you're programmed to see.
—Earl Hipp

The amazing thing about a good life partner list is that it will help you automatically focus your attention on the "right" person. Also, because of the chemistry in "noticing," your reaction to this person will be quite apparent . . . to both of you. As you become increasingly aware that he or she is a great fit with your list, your enhanced attention is a signal to them that they have something you want. If they feel the same way, your attention will quickly be reflected back. This is called flirting, and it's where the sweet dance of romance begins.

There is transformational power in list making. There is also a "right time" to start making your list. Keep reading to discover whether today is the right time in your life to start a life partner list.

Your Relationship to Relationship Assessment

To get ready to go on to the next chapter, take a moment to think about where you are, in this moment, in relationship to a prospective life partner.

Put a check mark next to the statement that best describes your current situation.

☐ I've been in a relationship for a while but I'm not sure this person is the right one.

☐ I've just ended a relationship and I'm still feeling the effects.

☐ I've been out of my last relationship a while now and want to do some dating. I'm not ready to look for a life partner yet.

☐ I've been dating for a while and I have just met a wonderful person who might be a good long-term prospect.

☐ I've been single for a while now. I like my life as it is, but I feel like this is a good time to add a life partner.

☐ Other.

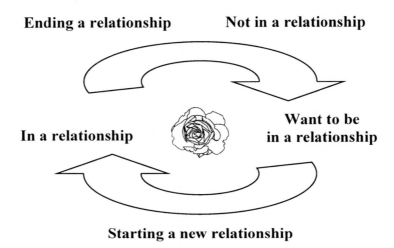

Ending a relationship　　**Not in a relationship**

In a relationship　　**Want to be
in a relationship**

Starting a new relationship

"I completed my list and then started feeling a little sad. I have been casually dating this guy I met three months ago. He's a good guy . . . but upon completing the list, I realized that he didn't have many of the qualities I valued in my MUST HAVE list. I realized that dating this guy—while fun to go to movies and stuff—wouldn't ultimately be satisfying in the long run. Damn. So I'm single again and paying closer attention to my list."

—Ted M.

The Best Time to Make Your List

Most single people inhabit the territory somewhere between the ending stages of the last relationship and the beginning stages of the next. The quality of the list you make and the energy you'll have for list making will vary greatly, depending on where you are on that continuum. While any well-thought-out life partner list is always better than just going on impulse or relying on your unconscious programming, if you fit into one of the following three categories you'll have some special challenges to consider.

Starting a New Relationship

Kim was excited to make her list but wondered if her timing was right. She explains, "I'm in the beginning stages of a new relationship. I think making my list now is very timely and will be helpful. Do you think my feelings for this new guy will get in the way of a good list?"

There is some danger in making your life partner list when you're dating someone new. You may want the relationship to work so badly you'll unconsciously manipulate your list to fit the new person. Another problem is if there are hints the person isn't really a fit, the rush of early romance combined with a little denial may cause you to avoid making a list at all. In Kim's case, it would have been better if she'd already had her list completed when she met her new friend.

I encouraged her to be brutally honest in her list making. I also pointed out that if she goes through all five steps in the list making process and is open to supportive objectivity from others, she will get the clarity she needs.

Digging out of a Past Relationship

If you're just out of a relationship, you may have some of the very common negative feelings that often result. You may feel a sense of personal vulnerability, left over feelings of anger about unresolved issues, and some hopelessness about ever finding the right partner. In this state, you can expect your life partner list to reflect your low levels of optimism and energy. Even in this condition, list making can be very helpful.

Steve, a few years out of a long marriage, used the list making process to help find his way back into the world of relationships. Steve said, "I had just begun making my life partner list when, almost immediately, I hit a huge wall of resistance. I had to stop and think over what I'd been living with since my divorce. I had to sort through my anger, need for self-protection, fear, isolating thinking and behaviors, and the frequent dreams about breaking free of my loneliness. I felt like one of those baby monkeys in the failure-to-thrive experiments. I hadn't been touched with loving thoughts, words, or hands for so long I didn't know if I ever would be again. I knew in my head and heart that living in the dark gray zone wasn't healthy and that I needed to make a mighty effort to break out. I was just lucky to find this process to help."

If you're still working your way out of the last relationship, it can take a heroic effort to find the energy to start anew. But many people have reported making their life partner list has hastened the return of optimism. In doing this work, you will be reminded that you deserve a good life partner. Your thinking about all the possibilities will give your optimism a jump-start—it will help you find the courage to move ahead with this important part of your life.

Your life partner list is a work in progress that will change as you learn more about yourself. If you can find the energy as you're digging out from the complicated feelings and old habits of a relationship ending, you may want to give the life partner list a shot. Even in difficult times, a little creative effort can increase your ability and desire to find love . . . on purpose.

One is such a lonely number.
—Madonna

Comfortable in Your Singleness

You'll make the very best list when you're feeling great about yourself—when you're comfortable in your singleness and you've decided this is the right time to add a partner to an already great life. That's when you'll have the most positive energy to do the considerable work involved in getting clear about your best life partner. You have this book in front of you for a reason. If you're comfortable in your life as a single person and feel this would be a good time to add a life partner to the mix, start now. Today, this moment, is the absolute best time to begin moving toward the life partner you want and deserve.

Regardless of where you are on the relationship continuum at this moment, if you feel you're ready to start making your life partner list, seize the moment and start now.

Seize the moment.
Man was never intended
to become an oyster.
—Theodore Roosevelt

My Promise to You

A life partner list is more important than any other list you'll ever make because of the enormous impact it will have on your life. But it will involve some work on your part. This is the "on purpose" part of *Finding Love On Purpose.*

If you take each of the five steps in order and spend the short time necessary for each step, you'll invest somewhere between three to five hours creating your list. Adding the suggested down-time between steps, you can easily complete the process in less than a week. This is a very small investment of your time and energy for such an important part of your future.

My promise to you is if you commit to finishing the process, the assignments will go quickly, be exciting, and teach you *a lot* about yourself. I promise you'll save enormous amounts of time and emotional energy that would have gone into relationship dead-ends. Most importantly, I promise that if you work through all the steps and create a solid life partner list, you will greatly increase the chances of finding exactly the life partner you have envisioned for yourself.

To further increase your chances of success, I suggest you make a commitment to yourself right now. Promise yourself you'll see the work described in this book through to completion. This important part of your life deserves the time and attention that creating your list requires. Make this promise to yourself because you deserve to find love on purpose and the best possible life partner.

You wouldn't be reading this far if you weren't ready to act. This book will provide the guidance, and the "right" person is out there waiting for you. With a solid commitment to yourself in place, it's time to start creating your life partner list.

Creating Your Life Partner List

The Process: In the sections ahead, you'll be taken through each of the five steps required to build a spectacular life partner list. To come out of this process with the best possible result, don't look ahead; take each step in order. You can always go back and change it later. Until the happy day when you find the right person and can put your list away for good, you'll be continually discovering, developing, and refining your collection of partner attributes. For now, just take it one step at a time, till you've completed the process.

IMPORTANT NOTE
You can stop your list development after completing any of the steps. At each of those points along the way you'll be much better prepared to recognize and attract the right life partner than you were previously. You may decide after step one that a simple and basic list is enough. If so, you'll be better off than when you were operating without a list. But the more steps you complete, the better your list, and the better the fit between you and the prospective life partners you find.

Consider your list to be "under construction" until you have completed the whole process. People have come back to continue their list making a month, a year, or a marriage later, but it's best to do a great job the first time. Both you and your list are works in progress, and will continue to evolve until you're in a relationship with the right person.

The Mechanics: Because of the number of changes you'll be making as you continually refine your life partner list, I highly recommend you create it in a word processor. It can be done on paper, but the many revisions and additions will work against your willingness and ability to keep going. It's best if you have both this book and a word processor document open at the same time. That way you can edit, cut, and paste attributes as your list evolves.

A Quick Note for the Technically Challenged: If the words "cut and paste" strike fear into your heart, here's a little help.

In most word processing programs you can "Cut" words from a document and then "Paste" them into another document or to a new location in the same document. You begin by highlighting the text you want to move. The easiest way to do this is to use your mouse to place the cursor at the beginning of the text you want to move. Then, while holding down the left mouse key, drag the highlight to the end of the text you want to cut. Then click the "Edit" menu and choose the "cut" option. Next, find the location where you want to insert your chosen text. Place the cursor at that location, return to the "Edit" menu and choose the "Paste" option. Magically the text will appear at the new location.

It's time to start, so fire up your word processor, create a document titled, "My Life Partner List," and let's begin.

First love is only a little foolishness
and a lot of curiosity.
—George Bernard Shaw

Step One: Creating Your Basic List

This is where the fun really begins. At this point, don't worry about making the perfect, all-inclusive list. In making your basic list, you're creating the raw material you'll shape into a more functional, refined, and complex list as you work through the steps. On making his first list, Dwayne said:

> As I made the list, I felt I was actually taking control of my unconscious list. I felt like I wasn't going to have to settle for just anyone. I liked being exact in asking for what I wanted. At the same time, it seemed to be too perfect of a scenario, and I worried about being unrealistic. I guess you could say I felt like I was laying down the first bricks on the path leading to my ideal partner but not sure where the path was going.

As in all creative projects, you must give yourself permission to make a rough draft. At this point in the process you're just developing a "wish list," and there is no need to edit or worry about being unrealistic. Hey, this is your life; why not ask for the best? You deserve that in a life partner.

It's way too early to be concerned with how you're going to turn this list into action. The important thing at this point is to do *something* . . . to start down the path that will lead to your best possible life partner.

Developing your basic list begins with simply making a list of all the attributes you want in a life partner.

Too much of a good thing is wonderful!
—Mae West

Starting Your Basic List

As you'll soon learn, you can create your list in any form that works for you. You can make a simple bulleted list, or you can use phrases like the following, and then fill in the blanks. If you use the statements like those just below, duplicate them a few times in your word-processing document before you start in order to make a long worksheet. Then it's time to start writing.

- ❤ My life partner has…
- ❤ My life partner likes to…
- ❤ My life partner is…
- ❤ My life partner will…
- ❤ My life partner is open to…
- ❤ My life partner regularly…
- ❤ My life partner knows how to…

Keep on saying these statements to yourself and record whatever comes to mind. In order to stay ahead of your inner critic, you'll want to write as fast as you can. You may even want to get a trusted friend to read these statements to you so you can stay focused, keep writing, and stay out of your analytical mind.

In making this basic list, don't be surprised at your responses. No matter how strange, funny, idealistic, or unattainable your list of attributes sounds, do not edit . . . just keep writing. You'll have plenty of opportunity to revise your list later. At this step, the goal is simply to create a list of attributes that will begin to paint a picture of your ideal life partner. Keep it fun and keep writing.

STOP reading now, open your word processor program, and create the "My Life Partner List" document. Enter the suggested statements from above, or just start listing life partner attributes. After you've created your initial list, look at the first drafts of the lists by Bill and Aimee that follow. From their examples, you can see that you're not engaged in a complicated writing project but having fun thinking about exciting possibilities.

Aimee's First List

You remember Aimee was the woman who ultimately had her list read by the best man at her wedding dinner to roast her new husband. When she created her basic list she was feeling hopeless about finding a life partner and could only vaguely describe what attributes she wanted. It was a huge effort for her to make any list, but today she's very glad she did. Aimee didn't use the suggested phrases; she simply titled her list "My Ideal Guy" and began to paint a word picture. Here's her first list:

My Ideal Guy

- Likes to laugh
- Adores me (opens doors, gives me flowers, surprises me, romances me)
- Approaches all things with a positive attitude
- Respects marriage
- Treats people with respect…especially his family
- He's 5' 10" or taller, and shouldn't be thinner than me
- Comfortable at a formal ball and a corner bar
- Likes to travel (explore)
- Can run a power tool if needed
- Wants to be a father
- Enjoys a beer or two
- Believes in a higher power (Catholic would be cool)
- Successful enough in business to have lots of time to play
- Money to play with would be nice too
- Nonsmoker
- Physically active (no couch potato)

With her basic list completed, Aimee had a great start and was having fun. Most importantly, her smile and her optimism about finding a great life partner were quickly returning.

Bill's First List

Bill is an eighty-year-old friend of mine in Tucson. He was four years past his wife's death when he began to think about female companionship, but he could barely think about dating. After a marriage of forty-three years, he wasn't at all ready for the notion of another marriage or "life partner," and simply wanted a woman friend. When I asked him what kind of woman he'd like to date, he said he didn't have any idea. I suggested he make a list describing the attributes his new companion might possess.

Like so many people who don't think they know what they want in a partner, Bill was a little unsteady initially. But when he actually began writing, a surprisingly detailed list began to emerge from the fog. Here's the description of what Bill called his "New Woman Friend."

Bill's New Woman Friend

- She is a Catholic woman over 65.
- She enjoys classical music and some opera.
- She is sensual, enjoys touching and sex.
- She enjoys travel and sightseeing.
- She is average build and my height.
- She is willing and able to be a good life partner.
- She is open and honest.
- She is a good listener.
- She is fair and reasonable when there are disagreements.
- She is a nonsmoker.
- She enjoys reading and occasional TV.
- She is healthy.
- She likes dogs.
- She is social.
- She is open to creating a life together.

- She is a good cook.
- She wants to live in a clean home.
- She attends church more than once a week.
- She is open to a relationship with my kids and grandkids.
- She wants to live in Arizona at least part of the year.
- She enjoys social drinking.

Not only did Bill come up with a great basic list, but the list making process helped him to seriously consider what it would be like to spend time with the woman he was describing. You could tell that his courage and hopefulness were growing along with the notion of becoming social again. We'll catch up with Bill later, but his list is another example of a good basic life partner list.

Regardless of the method used to create your list, at this point you'll want to put it in a workable form. In the steps ahead, you'll be working with each of your list items individually and it will be much easier if they are separated. Like Bill and Aimee, arrange your list so you have one attribute per line.

Before going on to the next step, let's tackle one more quick activity that may help you add a few more items to your basic list. I call it "Mining the Gold."

Mining the Gold in Your History
In addition to all the positive attributes you listed on your first life partner list, you will probably have some notions about what you don't want to see in a life partner. Being in relationships that didn't work out and being hurt a few times in difficult endings can leave you with strong feelings about certain characteristics in a partner. With that in mind, there is a way you can benefit from your downside relationship experiences by *briefly* considering the attributes you *don't* want in a life partner.

Let's start the process of mining the gold by opening a new word processor document and titling it "Negative Life Partner Attributes." You can just start remembering and writing, or, as you may have done before, create a bulleted list with phrases such as:

- I don't want a life partner who . . .
- I don't want a life partner who won't . . .
- I don't want a life partner who likes . . .
- I don't want a life partner who doesn't like . . .
- I don't want a life partner who is not open to . . .
- I don't want a life partner who feels . . .
- I don't want a life partner who can't . . .
- I don't want a life partner who believes . . .
- I don't want a life partner who has . . .
- I don't want a life partner who allows . . .

Use these phrases in the same way you did when you were thinking about positive life partner attributes by completing the statements. This exercise may churn up a lot of old and negative feelings that can leave you de-motivated, so don't overdo it.

> *I never hated a man enough*
> *to give his diamonds back.*
> —Zsa Zsa Gabor

Simply take a few moments to consider what elements of your past relationships didn't work for you and add those items to this list. You'll want to save the results from this activity. You'll be returning to them when we talk about "Deal Breakers" later in the process.

A functional life partner list must have a positive tone and focus on what you want in a life partner, not what you want to avoid. So you'll use these downside attributes in a constructive way by turning them into "gold."

Start by taking each of the negative statements and restating it as a positive. For example, take the statement, "I don't want a life partner who is cheap" and change it into, "I want a life partner who is generous," or something similar. After you've turned the negative into a positive statement, check to see if that positive attribute is already on your basic list. If you don't find it, add it. Continue this process with each of your negative attributes until you've turned them all into "gold" and added the missing items to your basic list.

This step can be challenging for two reasons. The first is that you have to use reverse thinking—considering what the opposite of a negative characteristic might be. The second and possibly more difficult challenge is that it takes you back to old memories, feelings, and hurts. Don't spend too much time in this dangerous territory, or feel free to skip it altogether if it's too hard. But there is "gold" in your relationship history if you can get to it.

When you've completed this second stage of list making, you'll have a substantial basic list. **Congratulate yourself!** Before going on, read through your list of positive life partner attributes. See what feelings come up for you. Like a developing Polaroid photo, a vision of your potential life partner is beginning to emerge from the background. As that happens, you'll begin to feel a growing excitement that will give energy to the rest of the steps.

The Emotional Undertow

At this point in your list development, you should know that in addition to the excitement, it's common to experience a little fear and some self-doubt. You've asked for what one person termed "the whole package." You've made an important and private part of yourself visible, and as a result, you're vulnerable. You have many of your hopes and dreams tied up in this list, and a powerful emotional undertow of complicated feelings is a very normal outcome. You should be a little disoriented now.

Steve's reaction to having completed his basic list expresses many themes common for first time list makers.

> I feel so clumsy and coarse. I want to say neat things and instead I come off to myself as . . . well, I can't put it into words but I feel like my list is just dumb! I think part of it is when looking at my list, I see things I want that feel unachievable. I want a person in my life whose presence will make my eyes dance and my heart sing. I want to feel safe with her.

> I want to meld spiritually, emotionally, and erotically with someone without fear. And that seems to be the key with me. I want to live without fear. Reading other people's lists, I have fear. The fears seem to be around my own perceptions of how lacking I am. I fear no one would want what I have to offer. And then there are the thoughts I have about the search for my beloved. I know she is present in this world but I have no idea how we will meet.

In his statement, Steve expresses a number of very common anxieties for basic list makers. After working with many people, I can report every list maker will, to some degree, experience some or all of the following feelings:

- ♥ I really don't know why I'm doing this.
- ♥ I really don't think it will work.
- ♥ I'm afraid this will work.
- ♥ How can making a list help me find a love relationship?
- ♥ I should just feel the chemistry with the right person.
- ♥ The person I'm describing is too perfect to be possible.

♥ I'm not sure I deserve someone this wonderful.

♥ If this person is out there, they won't be interested in me.

These concerns are very normal and you will learn to deal with them all as you make your way through the remaining steps. For now, know it's OK to feel uncomfortable, emotionally confused, and unsure . . . but that's not a reason to stop creating your list. In the steps ahead, you will continue to refine your list, gain objectivity, increase your confidence, and find supportive friends.

Give yourself a huge pat on the back for the work you're doing to improve your life by setting out to find love on purpose. Then take a little time off (you decide how much) to let things calm down a little. When you feel ready, go on to step two.

To love is to suffer. To avoid suffering one must not love. But then one suffers from not loving. Therefore to love is to suffer, not to love is to suffer. To suffer is to suffer. To be happy is to love. To be happy then is to suffer. But suffering makes one unhappy. Therefore, to be unhappy one must love, or love to suffer, or suffer from too much happiness.
I hope you're getting this down.
—Woody Allen

Step Two: Adding Breadth to Your List

At this point, your basic life partner list will likely be fairly short. In addition, the list will be a mix of impulsive, hopeful, serious, and playful attributes that reads like a wish list. But because you can assume you're going to get a lot of what you ask for on your list, you'll want to be sure you've covered a broad range of life partner attributes and haven't forgotten anything important. In this step, you'll review your basic list and spend some time thinking about attributes you may have missed in the first step that you'll want to be sure to include.

My guess is about now you'd like to see a template including all the crucial attributes every good life partner list should have. The problem with any examples I could provide is they would take away the excitement of discovering the characteristics that are most important to you. It's a safe bet the attributes on Bill's or Aimee's list won't do much to inspire your life partner search. That's because what really gives your list the energy it needs to work in your life is that you uncover the attributes that speak to you, and that you record them in your own words.

> *People shop for a bathing suit with more care*
> *than they do a husband or wife.*
> *The rules are the same.*
> *Look for something you'll feel comfortable wearing.*
> *Allow for room to grow.*
> —Erma Bombeck

Before going on, open your basic life partner list document and read through it. Try to imagine yourself spending time with the person your list describes. As you explore this vision, see if you can come up with additional attributes which create some excitement for you.

As this activity unfolds, you may find yourself having the "oh yeah's." That's when you say to yourself, "oh yeah, my partner should also have . . . ." Remember, adding breadth still isn't about making the perfect list. This step is about making sure your list includes a lot of what you want in a life partner and that it generates excitement for you. To help you broaden your list just a little more, let's consider three other sources of inspiration: other people's relationships, the things you value, and what the media teaches us about life partners.

Other People's Relationships

One good place to look for additional attributes for your list is to consider other people's relationships. Start with a friend who's in a relationship you admire. As you think about your friend and their partner, consider how they relate to each other, what they do together, or what they stand for as a couple that looks good to you. Try this with a few different couples. Each of them will have different strengths and problems that will suggest unique partner attributes for your list.

Common Values

Another approach is to consider the values you and your life partner would share—what common beliefs, interests, practices, or preferences would help you and your partner make choices when it comes to:

> Giving to charity
> Owning a home
> Having children
> Expressing your faith
> Deciding on vacations
> Getting a pet
> Managing money
> Buying new or used cars
> Agreeing on how the toilet paper comes off the roll
> (sometimes the little stuff is important)

Envisioning what would be important to you and your partner, how you'd live together, make decisions, and move through your life, may suggest additional important partner attributes for your list.

The Media
Countless books and magazine articles have been written on the topic of mate selection and various "must have" attributes for attracting and living with a life partner. In the movies you may see couples interact and be inspired to add something to your list. Watching television talk shows, soap operas, programs that offer relationship help, and dating programs will all expose you to examples of good, bad, and ugly partner attributes that may help you build your list.

After making the additions to your list, review it in its entirety again. A good list will have you smiling and your head nodding in the affirmative. You'll be having feelings of clarity, focus, and optimism just like a list maker named Anne.

Very Important Note!
As life partner lists are developed, they have a tendency to get longer and more detailed. For that reason, the working examples of people's life partner lists will be found in "The Lists" section starting on page 90. When it's time, you will be pointed to the appropriate page. Now let's get back to Anne's list.

Anne's Basic List
Anne is another list maker who, about four years out of her twenty-six-year marriage, decided she was ready for a new life partner. She had played around with dating, had fun and some interesting experiences, but she felt she wanted something more permanent. With hardly any effort, Anne quickly came up with a great basic list. To see Anne's basic list go to page 91.

On completion of her basic list Anne wrote, "I can't believe it! I DID IT!!!! Do you think he will show up tonight at 7:30?"

As Anne's e-mail list coach, I told her she had created a very good list and was getting closer to meeting this man, but 7:30 might be a bit quick. Then I pushed Anne to broaden her list. I asked her if her prospective partner could live in Mexico because she hadn't included a statement about where he was located. She didn't mention age, so I asked her if he could be seventy-five with "kids" in their forties. I asked her who, in her circle of friends, had a great relationship and what did she like about how they interacted. In addition to dancing, going to church, and giving and receiving "snuggles," I asked what else the two of them might do together. Anne came back with the following:

> You are right on about what's missing. When I read your note I said to myself, sheez, this list is getting too long. But then I really didn't want to leave any of the important things out. So here are the additions to my list:

> I'd like him to be between forty-five and sixty years old. His kids can be any age, but I prefer them to be beyond the teenage years. When I think about it, I really don't have a particular religion preference, but if he would go to St. Luke's (Catholic) Church with me that would be neat.

> He HAS to live within thirty minutes of my home (well, I guess I narrowed that down!). We will travel together to Ireland, Italy, France, Asia, Africa, the Northwest and Northeast, We'll hike together, ride horses, rock climb, bike, rollerblade, walk, read, explore, cook, eat, drink, and be merry together. I guess he has to fit into my life.

We'll see Anne's expanded list just ahead. Once she was pushed a little, her imagination came alive, and she rapidly added attributes to her list. She began to see herself with the man her list was describing. When I asked her how her list made her feel, she replied, "I FEEL excited, smart, energized, focused, centered—you know what? I don't feel scared at all! Pretty darn good!"

Seeing Partner Attributes—Everywhere

After all this brainstorming, it's time for you to take a break and stop actively working on your list or even reading this book. Simply bask in the glow of your success to this point. For now, put your life partner list away, and go about your life . . . but do carry a little notebook and pen.

Because you've been concentrating on attributes, your list will float around in the back of your mind and selective perception will be operating. As you move through your daily life, you'll find items for your list will come to you out of nowhere. You could be in a fast-food restaurant and see a kid with greasy hair working behind the counter and suddenly realize you want to put "good personal hygiene" on your attributes list. You'll be in line at the grocery store and see a couple fighting and decide you want a person who "fights fair and isn't mean." Anne tells the story of how she came to have an interesting attribute on her list.

> I was watching my new guy friend play with his new puppy, rolling around on the floor. I was thinking I really like this guy's playful spirit and gentle nature and made a note to add those to my list. All of a sudden, the puppy started licking him all over the face and he was making motions like he was kissing the puppy back . . . I mean their tongues were touching! I found myself totally grossed out thinking he'd try to kiss me good-bye with those same lips. When I got home I added, "Doesn't let dogs lick his face" to my list.

Knowing When to Stop

If you've been following the instructions and adding breadth to your life partner list, you're discovering the problem isn't about having enough list items, but that it's hard to *stop* seeing desirable partner attributes. When you're fully engaged in list making, it seems as though there is always one more item you just have to add. Somewhere along the way, you're simply going to have to decide your list is good enough and choose to stop.

When you feel it's time, add any remaining items, then close the "My Life Partner List" document and consider the second step finished.

As I stated earlier, you could stop the list making process at this point and you'd be clearer about your prospective life partner than you ever were before you started. However, completing three more steps will greatly enhance the quality, functionality, and power of your list. When you feel your list has sufficient breadth, you're ready for the next and very important step—discovering which partner attributes are the *most* important.

Love is a fire.
But whether it is going to
warm your heart
or burn down your house,
you can never tell.
—Joan Crawford

Step Three: Deciding What's Important

I think you'll agree not all of the attributes on your list are equally important. It might be nice if your prospect likes dogs or drives a Chevy truck, but actually being single and available for a relationship just might be more important to you. In this step, we'll sort your list in two different ways. The goal is to get fierce clarity about which attributes are really the most important to have in your life partner. You're going to love the result.

The Three-Category Sort

The three-category sort asks you to separate your current list of attributes into three groups of varying degrees of importance. Open your most recent "My Life Partner List" document, and then rate each attribute according to the following scale:

♥ **A = Absolutely Required** attribute in my life partner

♥ **I = Important** attribute, but not absolutely required in my life partner

♥ **N = Nice to Have** attribute, but if I really had to, I could live without this in my life partner

Expect to have some confusion about how to categorize some of your attributes, but don't let the confusion stop you. Facing the hard choices now will give you confidence later when you have to make difficult decisions about a *nice* person with *some* desirable traits . . . and that time will come. While the positions of various attributes may shift over time, your sorted list will represent the most important life partner attributes more clearly than your basic list.

> *I want a man who's kind and understanding.*
> *Is that too much to ask of a millionaire?*
> —Zsa Zsa Gabor

Start the sort by looking through your list for those attributes you feel are "Absolutely Required" in your life partner and place an "A" in front of them. When you've gone through the whole list, use the cut and paste method to group all the "A" items together at the top of the document. Some list makers will even highlight these attributes by changing the font color to symbolize their degree of importance.

Continue the sort with the remaining items, deciding whether each attribute is either "Important" or simply "Nice to Have." Place the appropriate letter in front of each attribute, and when you're done, move those items into common groups. When you've completed this activity, your life partner list will be divided into three categories: "Absolutely Required Attributes," "Important Attributes," and "Nice to Have Attributes."

Anne's First Sorted List
In step one Anne created a basic list, and then in step two she added a few additional partner attributes to give her list more breadth. In step three, when Anne attempted to sort the attributes by importance, she had a hard time deciding which attributes were very important and which would be just nice to have. She wanted her life partner to have *all* the attributes on the list and, as a result, almost everything became "Absolutely Required." She had only four items in the "Important" category and just one in the "Nice to Have" category.

To see Anne's first sorted list go to page 93 in "The Lists" section of the book.

It's all right to hold out for everything on your list . . . if you're prepared to hold out for a very long time. A much better strategy is to really push yourself to make tough choices, and then see how your list feels. You might want to get a trusted friend to help you be objective about where to put list attributes.

Anne's Second Sorted List

When I first challenged Anne about all of the "Absolutely Required" items on her list, she resisted any further sorting. "I am clearly picky," she responded. "Wait, no I'm not. I'm just asking for a lot. I'm sure it has to do with the significant reflection I've been going through since my divorce." But with a little push, Anne went back to the drawing board and came up with a second sorted list. Having a friend work with you during the tough parts of list sorting can really help. To see Anne's second sorted list go to page 96 in "The Lists" section.

As you can see, Anne still has a lot of "Absolutely Required" attributes, but forcing herself to make some tough choices has really paid off. She has more clarity about what's truly important.

Before continuing, be sure you have pushed yourself to make the hard decisions. When your three-category sort is finished, you'll know not only what attributes you're looking for in a life partner, but which attributes really are the most important.

There is one additional activity to finish this step and to bring your definition of what is truly important into very sharp focus. It's called "Putting First Things First."

Putting First Things First

Prioritizing your life partner list is the next important activity. Most list makers get a lot of what they ask for in a life partner, but few are lucky enough to get every single item. Rest assured, the time will come when you'll meet someone with many, but not all, of the attributes you want in a partner. When you do, you're going to have to ask yourself the very difficult question: Is there *enough right* about this person to continue to invest my time and energy? This is such a difficult call for so many singles, we'll give this topic its own chapter later in the book.

To make it easier for you when that moment arrives, it's very important to take the time now, when you can be objective, to get what I call fierce clarity about which attributes on your sorted list are the most important. If you don't prioritize your list in this way, you're more likely to act on impulse if you're in a needy mood and you encounter a person who has *some* things you want.

> *Love is like an hourglass,*
> *with the heart filling up*
> *as the brain empties.*
> —Jules Renard

You've already done a lot of work to sort your list and, like Anne, you'll be tempted to take the easy road and skip this activity. But if you're willing to look at the attributes closely, you'll realize they really do have varying degrees of importance for you. Force yourself to stay with this challenge, dig deep to find the prioritizing energy, and make those difficult choices. If you do, I can promise you on the day when the person who has *some* of what you want shows up, you'll be very grateful.

Your assignment is to open your list document and arrange the list items, in each of the three categories, from most to least important. Start with the "Nice to Have" category because it should be the easiest. Read through the items in that section of your list and choose the single most important attribute. Move it to the top of the "Nice to Have" section. Now go back through the remaining items in this category and find the next most important attribute, and place it just below the first. Continue until your "Nice to Have" items are listed in order from the most to least important . . . Really! Stop now and actually DO it.

Now that you know the process, continue to prioritize the "Important" and, finally, the "Absolutely Required" sections. The "Absolutely Required" section will be the most challenging but will provide the most guidance when it's finished.

When you've finished this step, every item in each of the three categories will appear in order of importance. At this point, you have a solid and functional list you can really put to work.

Bill and Anne approached the prioritizing assignment in very different ways. To see Anne's sorted and prioritized list go to page 99 in "The Lists" section.

Bill had the extra challenge of working on paper instead of a computer, but fortunately, his list was much less complicated. When I asked him to sort his life partner list into categories and then prioritize the items, he divided it into two sections. He described the "Absolutely Required" attributes as "Must Have," and put all the remaining attributes into a "May Have" category. Sorting his list into the two groups and then putting the list items in order of importance took him only fifteen minutes. This was a slightly different approach to the assignment, but it really worked for him. For Bill's sorted and prioritized list go to page 102 in "The Lists" section.

Bill chose to use his prioritized list as the basis for an ad in the singles section of a Tucson community entertainment paper. It really paid off. As of this moment, he's received a couple dozen letters, decided that twelve of the women fit his list, and had three dates. Bill is quite excited and treats the letters like money in the bank. He's taking his time to get over his shyness and having a lot of fun in the process.

With step three completed you know, without question, what attributes are important to look for when you set out to find love on purpose. In step four, you're going to learn about the power in the details. You'll learn how to bring your list to life in a way that will energize and drive your life partner search. In step four, your ability to find love on purpose will get its power.

Step Four: Adding Life to Your List

At this point you have a solid and reliable list. It's been sorted, prioritized, and it's beginning to be a very clear picture of your best life partner. However, in its current form your list is more a collection of descriptive attributes than a compelling vision of a relationship with the person of your dreams. Having a great list is a necessary, but somewhat intellectual, process. Step four will put the heart and passion in your list.

My Adobe Hacienda

If I were looking for a house instead of a life partner, step four is where I would move from saying, "It would be nice to have a big adobe house in Tucson, Arizona," to saying, "I will have a four-thousand-square-foot home on a five-acre lot in the northeast section of Tucson, Arizona. The house will be a one-story, terra-cotta-colored structure made of adobe, with a three-car garage. It will have three bedrooms, a screened veranda, and a den for my office. There will be a beehive fireplace in the dining area and a fully equipped professional kitchen with granite countertops. The house will be situated on the property in a way that offers a vista of the Catalina Mountains from the big picture windows and the patio. The grounds around the patio will be landscaped with a variety of cactus, decorated with sand-colored rock, and there will be lots of bird feeders. A lush bougainvillea vine, with bright red flowers, will climb the surrounding adobe wall."

Are you getting the idea? Reading this description of the home I'd like in Tucson helps me to see myself relaxing on the patio, looking up at the mountains in the evening, possibly having a frozen strawberry margarita . . . no salt . . . in a blue-stemmed glass . . . and maybe a cigar.

Filling in the small details moves you from a list of attributes to a compelling and life-giving vision of what you want.

The Power in the Details

A major benefit of adding details to your list is what happens
to you when you read it. When I go over the detailed description
of the Tucson house I want (and I have a lot more detail I didn't
include here), I can see it very clearly in my mind. I get excited,
energized, and drawn to that image. In the same way, the richness
that comes from the details you add to your life partner list will
generate a strong image of your prospective life partner and a
powerful vision of your life together. This final step requires the
most work, but you'll absolutely love the results.

If you take another look at Bill's sorted and prioritized list
(page 102), you'll notice he had more to say about some attributes
than others. For example, he said, "She is healthy . . . she won't be
in the early stages of a long-term illness, with all the caretaking
and the wear and tear on people that it can lead to." Instead of just
a few words about the attribute, he wrote a short but descriptive
sentence. Like Bill, you may have found some of your list items
have already started to grow into more detailed descriptions.

Adding detail to all your list attributes is the next natural,
critical, and final construction step in the evolution of your life
partner list. In this activity, you're going to be expanding each of
your short attribute descriptions by writing a sentence (or more)
about what each attribute means to you.

Think of what you'd say if you were trying to explain a list
item to someone else. For example, instead of just writing "He
likes kids," you'll want to jot down a few things about what that
means to you. Does "He likes kids" mean other people's kids,
kids who have left home, adult "kids," or infants? Does it mean
he wants his own kids? Does it mean he's a schoolteacher or camp
counselor? Does it mean your house will be the meeting place for
the kids in the neighborhood, or you'll open a store at the mall
selling kids clothing? What do *you* mean when you say, "He likes
kids?"

Assumptions are the termites of relationships.
—Henry Winkler

Over the course of my list coaching, I've come across many lists with three-word attribute descriptions. But when pushed for detail, almost everyone discovers there are tons of additional ideas, more complete thoughts, and amazing depth of vision about what their prospective partner will be like. Here are a few examples of some common attribute descriptions I've encountered and the type of questions that will bring out the necessary details.

He has money.

Does this mean the prospect should have money saved? Is the total amount of money the person has important? Do you want the person to be able to talk about money (hard for many people), have good money management skills, have family money, be generous with money, be good at making money, or does having a checkbook or enough money for beer qualify?

She is fit and healthy.

Does this mean you want a woman who has a regular physical activity program or just bikes to the gas station for cigarettes? Should she be a runner, walker, or someone who buys fitness equipment on late-night television? Do you want the person to be free of significant health problems? Do you require a certain body type or weight? Do you want a person who gets annual physicals or just has health insurance?

He is available.

Does available mean he lives close by, has a cell phone, or that he can carry on a reasonable conversation with occasional eye contact? Does available mean he has been divorced three years or more or would it be okay if he was in the process of divorce and only spends two nights a week at his wife's house? Do you want a man who owns his own home, stays with three college buddies, or is it all right if he's living with his mom?

When I initially asked Anne to add details to her prioritized list, she didn't think it was necessary. But once she got rolling, she was surprised about how much extra information she had to offer. As the details accumulated, she decided her list was even more exciting. To see Anne's detailed list go to page 104.

With this activity, Anne's list was finished . . . for now. When I asked her how it felt to have her list completed, she replied, "Five years ago, I had a male friend who was freshly divorced like me. He said he knew exactly what he wanted in a woman the next time around and he was going to get it. I said he was lucky, because I didn't know what I wanted and it made me sad. After finishing my list, I'm thinking RIGHT ON GIRL; you FINALLY KNOW what you want! I can actually visualize him and our life together, and now I'm ready to go find this guy!"

If you haven't already done so, open your "My Life Partner List" document, pick an attribute, and begin to write a sentence or two. As you push yourself to add detail to your attributes, you'll most likely discover you have a lot to say about each one. If you have difficulty, this is another activity where the help of a trusted friend will make a huge difference. That person can draw you out, ask clarifying questions, and help you sustain your interest as you move through the list. Most importantly, your friend will push you for details and keep you writing.

Living the Vision
With this activity, you're programming your partner search engine with the details that will form a coherent vision and bring your list to life with emotional energy. Like the Tin Man in *The Wizard of Oz*, you're giving your list a heart, and it should stir up a mix of positive feelings when you read through it.

If you've completed all the steps, your list will read like a good novel or a script for a great movie that paints a romantic portrait of you in a relationship with your life partner.

That vision changes you in subtle ways. It changes what you project when you walk into a room and creates the energy people feel when they hear you describe your list. The picture in your mind and its emotional power is the force that will keep you moving confidently toward your life partner . . . for whatever time it takes.

You can renew your life partner search energy by revisiting your list at regular intervals. High-performance athletes will rehearse a vision of a successful performance in their minds as a regular part of their training. In the same way, you will benefit from mentally visualizing your partner and your life together as described in your list . . . daydreaming, on purpose, about the joys, satisfactions, and the sweetness of being with that person. In doing so, you are having a direct influence on the quality of the person you're going to meet.

At this moment, the future of your relationship life is truly in your hands. The amount of effort you put into this exercise is up to you. But if you are truly going to find love on purpose, make sure you have sufficient detail to generate a motivating vision of both your life partner and your lives together. If this wonderful vision makes you happy now, it will continue to make you happy when it becomes reality.

Speaking of adding details, I want to be sure to mention that on the patio at my Tucson home I will have a round, in-ground Jacuzzi with blue accent tiles. From there, I will be able to see a desert landscape, relax into the fragrance of the nearby lemon tree when it blooms in the spring, and see the moon as it comes up over the mountains. Because I'm going to get something very close to my vision, I didn't want to leave anything out.

Your life partner list is finished, although I'm sure you'll occasionally make changes as you head out to find love on purpose. You're ninety-eight percent of the way home now, with one very easy but very necessary activity standing between you and stepping out into the world. I think of this last task as getting an emergency brake.

Naming the Deal Breakers

I love my Subaru and I trust the car, but in case of a crisis, I still feel more comfortable having an emergency brake next to my right hand. Before you take your list into the world in step five, you'll want to add an emergency brake to your tool kit.

A deal breaker is any attribute in a person which makes him or her an *absolute* no-go for you. These are the terribly important and most often negative characteristics, which, if present, would cause you to pull on the emergency brake and walk away from a prospect, *even if that prospect has many desirable attributes*. Having this list handy will help position you for prime time.

Remember when you were making your basic list in step one and took a little time to think about what you *didn't* want in a life partner? At this point, it's time to return to your "Negative Life Partner Attributes" list and use it to create a very short list of deal breakers you can use as your emergency brake.

While this list is very personal, a few deal-breaking examples I've seen in my list-coaching experience include:

- Smoker
- Has young kids
- Not single
- Has a snake
- Drinker
- No money

- ⊘ Not my political party
- ⊘ Chronic illness
- ⊘ Wears leather
- ⊘ Hasn't done therapy
- ⊘ Drives a bus
- ⊘ Has pimples
- ⊘ Lives on a farm
- ⊘ Is gassy
- ⊘ Eats with his fingers
- ⊘ Snores
- ⊘ Poor hygiene
- ⊘ Lives too far away
- ⊘ Visible tattoos
- ⊘ Allows dogs to lick his face

When you're feeling needy and you encounter someone with some, or even a lot, of what's on your life partner list, you might be tempted to overlook a few glitches that really are important to you in the long run. That's when you should apply the emergency brake. Having made a list of deal breakers and a promise to walk away from a person if these attributes are present, you have a good first line of defense when the otherwise very nice person appears . . . and that will happen.

With your "Negative Life Partner List" as a guide, list up to ten big turnoffs, negative behaviors, no-nos, or screen-outs that are deal breakers for you. I suggest you write an introductory statement such as the one Anne used to describe her "No-Way" list. This is how Anne stated her intention: "Regardless of how attractive a person might be, I will walk away from anyone who has any of the following characteristics."

Your list of deal breakers will be different from Anne's, but the firmness and brevity of her short list makes it a good model. Here is Anne's list of "No-Way Factors."

Anne's No-Way Factors

Regardless of how attractive a person might be, I will walk away from anyone who has any of the following characteristics:

- ⊘ Smoker/drug user
- ⊘ Addictive behavior
- ⊘ Bad breath
- ⊘ Broke
- ⊘ Mean
- ⊘ Reckless
- ⊘ Criminal attorney
- ⊘ Lion tamer
- ⊘ Racist
- ⊘ Married

Two men (or two women) dating is different from a man and woman. In addition to asking some of the same questions, I have some others that need to be answered. For example, how out-of-the-closet are they and how much internalized homophobia will I accept.

—Ted M.

With your fully evolved life partner list and your collection of deal breakers in hand, it's time to ease into the world and put your list to work. A great way to start is to contact some of the people you trust the most and ask them for their support and objectivity. I call this activity, "Creating Your Relationship Team."

Step Five: Creating Your Relationship Team

Unless you've already called on your friends for support and assistance, you have been creating your life partner list in private. Now it's time to put out the call to a few of the people you trust and to form a relationship team.

Forming Your Relationship Team

Inviting others into your process at this point serves two very important goals. The primary reason to involve your friends is that they know you very well and can offer valuable and most likely needed objectivity about your list. In the same way writers have editors and companies have boards of directors, you can benefit from your friends' unique perspectives.

When you pull your relationship team together, you'll have a safe and informed group of trusted allies who can support you in finding love on purpose, both in the development of your life partner list and in those happy days when you're sorting through prospects.

The second reason to get others involved is when you share your list with them, you're taking the important first step of telling people what you want in a life partner. You'll be letting others know you're actively looking for a partner and asking for their help. You'll have to step out at some point, so why not use people you trust to get started?

As important as this step is, for some people, sharing their list with others makes them feel a little awkward. After all, your list contains a description of your most personal hopes and dreams. If this activity makes you uncomfortable, be extra careful about whom you choose to ask for support. The key is to pick people you can count on to treat you and your information with care and respect.

Don't short yourself and skip this step out of fear or shyness. When you find the courage to share your list with others, I can guarantee you'll find most people are more than happy to help. Most likely, they'll be amazed at your self-commitment and want to know all about how this process works.

Putting Your Team to Work

You can do this assignment any way that's comfortable for you. You might choose a "best" friend or two, a family member, or even a therapist for a trial run. At the other extreme, I know of a person who held a List Launch party with more than twenty people invited. Whatever your approach, tell your team what you've been up to and why. Tell them what you've learned about your desired life partner's attributes. Explain the importance of their feedback and ask for their support. Then share a copy of your list with them and ask them the following questions:

- ♥ Are there any attributes on my list you don't understand that I can clarify?

- ♥ What's missing? What should be on this list that I've forgotten to include?

- ♥ Can you see me with this person? Why or why not?

- ♥ Finally, ask them the big one: Do you know someone who is a fit with the attributes on my list?

As a result of their responses to your questions, you will very likely improve the quality of your list. In addition, it can't hurt to give your relationship team a little training on your list of desired life partner attributes. Because of the exposure to your shopping list, someone could soon be introducing you to a great prospect. At the absolute minimum, you will have begun the process of taking your list out into the world.

If you're not ready to go public with your list, but still want some feedback, you can send an e-mail to:

Coaching@FindingLoveOnPurpose.com.

You'll get a reply with information about my on-line, list-coaching services. While I won't have the benefit of knowing you, I've seen lots of life partner lists and I'll be happy to offer general feedback.

When possible, I'm putting together small groups of on-line list makers for mutual support via e-mail. Whether you're using your own support team, me as an e-mail coach, or a group of anonymous on-line pals, the objectivity and support trusted allies can provide will be invaluable as you create and then go public with your list.

That's it! Your list is completed and your support people are in place. Your movie is scripted: it's powerful, and it makes you happy. Now it's time to find your co-star. It's time to head out to find love on purpose.

Many of life's failures
are people who did not realize
how close they were to success
when they gave up.
—Thomas Edison

*Life shrinks or expands
in proportion to one's courage.*
—Anais Nin

*Security is mostly a superstition . . . .
Avoiding danger is no safer
in the long run than outright exposure.
Life is either a daring adventure,
or nothing.*
—Helen Keller

Taking Your List into the World

With a clear vision of a relationship with your life partner cooking away in the background, the only remaining question is *when* this person is going to show up in your life. Your person *is* out there, and you will be happy to know he or she is looking for you too. However, unless you get a lot of packages delivered at home and are looking for people who drive delivery trucks, the chances of your life partner knocking on your door any time soon are slim to none.

Taking your list into the world is all about taking charge of your relationship life and going after what you want. Being in charge means accepting responsibility for what happens. It means being proactive instead of playing the passive victim and simply reacting to the people you encounter by chance.

If you needed a new car, you wouldn't wait for someone to park the car of your dreams with a "For Sale" sign in front of your house. Instead, you'd spend some time thinking about the car that would fit your lifestyle today, do a little research, decide what you want, visit the dealers that sell the models you like, and maybe even test-drive a few that fit the bill. Why not bring that kind of intentionality to your search for a life partner?

> *Why do you sit there looking like an envelope*
> *without any address on it?*
> —Mark Twain

If you brought your friends and other trusted allies together on a relationship team in step five, you've got a start at moving into the world with your list. In fact, you may already be experiencing the benefits. The following seven strategies represent a continuum of approaches which move from very general to extremely direct approaches for finding a life partner who has just what you want. Each method has pros and cons, but they are all about being in the world with the intention of finding love, very much on purpose.

Whichever strategy you use, you should expect some initial discomfort as you develop your partner-searching skills. If you're like most list makers, you'll be out of practice at meeting people. It will take some courage to get started, but soon your confidence, along with your list of good prospects, will gradually increase. As your experience grows, you'll most likely want to move to the more direct approaches. You can certainly do whatever works for you, but please, do something. A good list is a terrible thing to waste.

Let's start with the least threatening approach to finding love on purpose . . . just being you and going about your business.

Going about Your Business
Just going about your business is the easiest but least direct approach to finding a life partner. It's almost a non-strategy because there's almost nothing extra you actually do. It simply involves your going about your daily routines, such as going to the coffee shop, working, picking up the dry-cleaning, buying your groceries, and exercising . . . but doing those things with your life partner list in the back of your mind.

This approach to finding your life partner works because *you* have changed as a result of your list making experiences. You understand yourself a little better, you're clear about the kind of person you're looking for, and you're seeing the people around you differently.

Without a life partner list, it's very easy to overlook someone who might be a great life partner candidate when that person is standing right in front of you. With your life partner list operating in the back of your mind, new prospects will suddenly become more obvious.

The fun part happens when you "notice" a person who you realize may be a fit with your list. Making eye contact, figuring out how and when to make a connection, and taking the time to get to know each other are all part of the romantic dance. As you go about your daily business, keep your life partner list in the back of your mind, and you'll notice your Geiger counter ticking when a good prospect is near.

To become just a little more intentional about your search, you can practice the win-win approach to social activity.

The Win-Win Approach to Social Activity

Perhaps you enjoy playing team sports, taking night school classes, campaigning for a political candidate, belonging to a gourmet cooking or book club, participating in organized bike rides, or attending lectures at your local museum. Being out in the world, doing the things you really enjoy, makes you and your life more interesting . . . and increases your chances of meeting a like-minded potential life partner.

Because you and your ideal life partner will ultimately have a number of common interests, there's a good chance you'll be drawn to similar events and locations. By pursuing a variety of interests, instead of spending your nights at home, you will greatly increase your chances of finding Mr. or Ms. Right. The win-win approach to social activity is if you're doing what you love and don't connect with a potential life partner, you still win because you're meeting interesting people, learning things, and becoming a well-rounded person.

Remember Anne's list? She wanted a partner who, like her, enjoyed rollerblading, going to church, cooking, dancing, and traveling. If Anne is going to practice the win-win approach to social activity, she might rollerblade regularly in a public place, join a rollerblading club, and go to an occasional rollerblade race. She'd worship regularly, possibly attending services at different churches. She may want to take cooking classes or dancing lessons, and her vacation plans might involve adventure travel for singles. You can see that even if Anne's guy doesn't show up, she'd have a fulfilling life . . . while keeping her partner search equipment operating at full speed.

Aggressively living a life you like, and meeting someone with a shared interest who might become a life partner candidate, is really great. It's also much better than simply going out for the sole purpose of meeting someone and then being disappointed when it doesn't happen. It's even better than just going about the business of your daily life because, when you meet someone while doing something you love, you instantly have something more interesting in common than the need to pick up your dry-cleaning.

There is a small problem with this approach, however. There's a chance your compatibility with a person may be limited to your common interest. While it can be great to meet someone who also likes rollerblading, for example, just having that in common may not be enough. He or she may not have enough of the other items on your life partner list to be a good prospect.

If you want to increase the chances of finding a person with more of your list attributes and leave even less to chance, you'll need to be just a little more intentional and a little more assertive about finding love on purpose. What follows are a number of ways you can directly ask the universe for exactly the person you want.

Asking Friends and Family

Your best friends and family represent a safe place to begin directly asking for what you want in a life partner. These people know you to some extent, think the world of you, and sincerely want you to be happy. They are always wanting to help, and they feel just about every single person they know would be a fit with you . . . because they are really nice and, well, they're single too.

As we discussed previously, if you simply turn your friends and family loose to find you a "nice person," you're setting your-self up for disappointment. The art in engaging this motivated sales force is to equip them with *your* shopping list. You can share your list with them in conversation, send it to them in an e-mail, or create a pocket-sized, laminated, handout version for their use. But unless your family and friends have solid guidance from you about the requirements for your life partner, you'll end up wasting a lot of time.

While the "Friends and Family" strategy has been successful for many, after enough mismatches you may just decide to be even more intentional. With the following approaches you'll be assertively putting your list to work and really taking charge.

Speed Dating

Speed dating, now available in most major cities, is a good way to increase your exposure in a hurry. It works something like this: An enterprising person qualifies a group of singles by some common denominator, like age, religion, or a common interest—and then gathers them all in the same room. To keep it safe and totally anonymous, each person is given a number instead of using names. When things start, you have ten minutes to "get to know" your first "date." You have to be quick because when the signal is given, regardless of your feelings about a person, you have to move on to the next person. This process continues until the event ends an hour or so later.

Think of the speed dating as paying a fee to have a dozen, very brief, and intense blind dates in an evening. At the end of the event, you tell the organizer the number of each individual you'd like to pursue. If those people are also interested in more time with you, contact information is then provided.

Speed dating can be a very efficient use of your limited partner-searching time and energy because it allows for a general screening of the people involved. Someone else does the work and gets a lot of candidates together in one place. It's safe, usually inexpensive, and takes only a few hours of an evening or after-noon. The best part is that because it's anonymous, you don't have to spend much time with someone who's not interesting.

The downsides of this approach are that anyone who meets the selection criteria for the group and can afford the cost of admission can become a participant. You may also find having a dozen or more brief conversations in an evening is exhausting. Speed dating works best if you can distill your life partner list into a series of clear questions you can ask under pressure. Think of it as an urban adventure because it certainly will be exciting.

If you've tried speed dating but it hasn't resulted in finding the love of your life, you may be ready to try an even more assertive approach for finding your life partner. The next three approaches involve directly going after exactly the person you want.

Advertising
Lots of people have successfully used the direct approach of placing an ad for a life partner in the "Personals" section of a local newspaper. According to Adweek, Americans spend $500 million annually on personal ads in newspapers and magazines alone. These short blurbs don't leave a lot of room for your full list, but if you focus on a few of the high-priority items from your "Absolutely Required" list, you'll have enough space to get started.

If you decide to try this approach, you may want to get your relationship team together to help you write your ad. While you'll be very clear about what you're looking for in a life partner, it'll be easier for your friends to come up with just the right words to sell you in the ad. Do make sure you make the final call on the ad's truthfulness because you're the one who has to live up to the advertising. After my friend Bill and I worked with his list for about fifteen minutes, we came up with an ad which brought him almost twenty responses—more than enough to keep him busy for quite a while.

You probably know someone who's met a life partner as a result of advertising. Ads are an inexpensive and anonymous way to get into the singles marketplace. Meeting and getting to know the people who respond to your ad will give you dating practice and a chance to put your life partner list to work as you screen prospects for the right attributes. If you're one of the lucky ones, your three-line invitation might blossom into a great life partner connection.

While advertising is a good way to directly ask for what you want, the problem is that it's a one-way street. You can put your specific request out in the world, but you won't know anything about the people who respond. Most likely, you'll spend a lot of time meeting people who answered your ad because *you* sounded good to them, but who aren't the least bit compatible with your life partner list.

If you get tired of all the work involved with meeting people who aren't "it," there's a way to pre-qualify prospects and save time by hiring someone to do the screening for you.

Matchmaking Services
Most major communities have many different services for singles who, for a fee, promise to match you and your interests with a like-minded person.

Using a face-to-face matchmaking or dating service can quickly increase the efficiency of your search and keep you from exhausting your limited partner-seeking energy. At sign up, you fill out a questionnaire explaining what you're looking for in a partner and be asked to describe yourself as clearly as possible.

To make a match, these services may use a computer or rely on employees who manually compare questionnaires. In theory, if both parties provide honest and detailed descriptions, and if the service really makes the match based on common criteria, you have a good chance of meeting a solid prospect on the first date. In some cases you'll be able to create a short video in which you describe yourself and who you're looking for. This approach helps a lot because you get to "meet" the person on screen before you decide if you want to meet them in person. Whatever the approach, if you're going to make a significant financial investment, be sure to check the service out with past customers.

Matchmaking services can be the perfect approach for busy people. When a match is made for you, you will be meeting someone else who has made finding a life partner a priority, and the two of you should also have a number of common interests. These services are more of a two-way street than personal ads because you know something about each other when you meet. You'll still have to screen for your most important attributes, deal breakers, and to make sure the person actually fits the description they supplied to the service. But the matchmaking service takes on the very hard work of finding you a person who has some, if not a lot, of what you want in a life partner prospect.

As helpful as these matchmaking services can be, many people are reporting that for much less money they are increasing both the number and quality of matches using one of the many on-line matchmaking services. Because of the power of computer technology, this approach to finding love on purpose can no longer be ignored.

On-line Matchmaking

An on-line search for the keyword "personals" instantly yields more than eight million responses from services who want to help you find the partner of your dreams. Harnessing the considerable technological power of computers and the extensive reach of the Internet really pumps matchmaking up a notch.

Today you can find on-line matchmaking services catering to specific interests. There are services that will match you with people who have a similar religious affiliation, people who like the same sports you do, or people from your political party. There is even a site for the "politically agitated," at *loveandwar.com.* They claim to be, "the social network for people who care about politics."

If you're OK with a search that's more general, the really big players in this on-line marketplace maintain huge databases of singles. This means you can compare your list to the those of millions of other on-line relationship seekers. Tim Sullivan, the president of match.com, one of the largest on-line matchmaking services, says, "A larger database makes for more personalized searches." As of this writing, Match.com has grown to more than twelve million members . . . and that represents a lot of potential matches.

Most big matchmaking websites offer free instant searches. They will also let you place a free ad complete with a photo and, in some cases, voice or video greetings. On most of these sites, you can post a detailed profile listing some of your personal data, including a narrative section describing both yourself and what you're looking for in an ideal match. Some sites will notify you of new and compatible listings by sending you an email or they will deliver the information to your cell phone to help you beat the competition to the door.

With a paid registration, you can do advanced searches, share your profile selectively, screen responses quickly, flirt in real time with an instant messaging program, and do it all while staying as anonymous as you like.

List maker Laura is using on-line matchmaking to find her life partner. She says, "I'm a member of match.com, and one of the aspects I like is I can anonymously post a profile. I can also place a search with the qualities I'm looking for in a partner and get the responses e-mailed directly to me with the qualifying profiles attached. I reply to every e-mail response I receive. When the profile doesn't match what I'm looking for, I kindly thank them for responding and wish them every success in meeting someone special. It's very efficient"

Just a few of the benefits of on-line matchmaking include:

- Getting exposure to people you'd never otherwise meet.

- Being as anonymous as you want and in complete control of what happens. You decide whom to send e-mail to and who deserves a response. If you sense something's not right, you simply hit the delete button.

- Participating when it's convenient. You can search for your partner candidates at any time, twenty-four hours a day. It is easy to hop on-line and search on Friday night, after the kids are in bed or at 3:00 A.M. if you're a night owl.

- Using e-mail. Because it's all done by e-mail initially, you can take your time getting to know someone. You get to decide when you're ready to take the next step of talking on the phone or meeting in person.

- Being able to search by zip code for prospects close to home.

- Saving money. Compared to in-person services or just going out for a night on the town, on-line services are inexpensive. Monthly fees range from $12.95 to $24.95 a month and there's usually a break if you commit to a longer term.

Try several on-line matchmaking services till you settle on one you like. You shouldn't have any trouble finding a place to start because entering the word "matchmaking" in just about any search engine will get you more than a million responses. Unless you're open to a long distance romance, try to find a service that allows you to search for singles in your geographic area.

Go slowly at first. When meeting on-line, as in the face-to-face world, you'll come across people who are dishonest and manipulative. Always protect your identity, and don't give out any personal information until the person has earned your trust. You have no reason to hurry, especially when a little on-line mystery can make the process more exciting.

After completing step three, "Deciding What's Important," Steve got so enthusiastic about his prospective life partner he joined an on-line matchmaking service. With his life partner list as a guide, he came up with a powerful statement of what he wanted in his life partner. His statement is a great example of how to be romantic, playful, and have fun with an on-line approach.

Steve's Dream Partner
The accompanying photo was taken in Siena during a three-week solo trip, when I skied Austria and saw Italy for the first time. The thought of traveling alone for that long was at first daunting, but along the way I learned that I like the way I approach my life and I that really do like me.

It was during that journey I became more ready than ever for important changes. Single for six years, I had arrived at a new place. A place in my life where there is at last room for another . . . for a beloved.

What I desire is in many ways what I am. I want a person my age or close (54 in June), who watches the back channels on TV, reads a lot, gives and receives foot and body rubs, and is quite uninhibited in private moments.

I am open to being married or not married, but I am committed to being in the relationship with a high degree of integrity. I seek a comfortable traveling companion. Someone who doesn't need to be highly scheduled; who can live out of a medium-sized backpack for fifteen days, and who is pleased by the adventure of being lost in the back streets of Rome, or Paris, or the hills of Tuscany.

I want truthfulness, fidelity, self-deprecating humor, and a person comfortable with silence and conversation. You have to love my dog, get past my slovenly housekeeping, and give me reasons to work fewer hours.

If it's going to work, we have to be mutually attracted on all levels. So an attractive face and body, well dressed and groomed, with a sense of fashion, is important. You'll need animation of expression, a love of touching (do you know Sweet Honey and the Rock's song "Seven Day Kiss?"), shared values, and a history with some relationship pain.

I also want a person with a sense of the sacred and most Sundays you will find me in church. Monday evenings are for my men's group. My politics are moderate to liberal. I cook, I bake, I have a garden, enjoy a libation at the end of the day, and own a closet full of guns that have not been fired in a long time. I have three kids in their twenties and a mom in her nineties; all of whom I love more than life itself.

So…that's me…what I want, need, and hope for. If you have courage to stay in a conversation when it's hard to do, can tell me what you need, be respectful of my spirituality, be grateful for what I am able to offer, have the integrity to seek what you need in the relationship, and have at least a little "shazamm". . . please respond.

If I can find you, I promise you will be adored.

If you've done the work to create a good life partner list, are clear about your deal breakers, and have some support, you're very well prepared for any of these approaches to finding love on purpose. Your only remaining challenges are all about knowing what to do when the right person shows up.

A bride at her second wedding
does not wear a veil.
She wants to see what she is getting.

—Helen Rowland

What to Do
When Your Person Shows Up

Meeting the person who is a great fit with your life partner list will actually feel quite different than your standard date. The major challenges in that meeting include actually recognizing that you're facing a hot prospect, and then making sure there's enough right about the person to open your heart to the experience. Of course, there's also the challenge of containing your enthusiasm while you get it all figured out, but that really is the fun part.

Recognizing Your Life Partner
So you'll know what to expect, here's a generic description of what a first encounter with the right person might be like.

You are at an event or doing something you enjoy and as a result you're in a good mood. You'll recognize your person when they come into view because you have created a vision of what he or she will look like. When you actually connect , you feel as if you're meeting someone you've known for a long time, and you'll almost immediately feel comfortable in their presence.

Very quickly you'll feel a rush of excitement as you begin to realize your new acquaintance has a lot of what you want in a partner. Because of your shared interests, the two of you will quickly discover you have a lot to talk about. The conversation will flow naturally, be interesting, and the pace will feel just right.

As your time together unfolds, you'll find yourself mentally referring to your life partner list. You'll have a growing awareness this person is a fit with your vision and you'll have a feeling of "correctness" as you get to know more about him or her. You'll feel an optimistic excitement developing and the time will fly. It will be hard not to move too fast and easy for the two of you to decide how and when to meet again.

What You'll Do after You Meet

When you return home, you'll get your life partner list and compare your new person with the vision you've created. You'll decide that this person is worth the investment of your time and emotional energy. You'll call someone on your relationship team to share the good news and get an objective opinion. Once you know, without question, you're on the right track, you'll allow yourself to feel the physical and emotional rush of early romance. You'll feel your heart opening to all the sweet possibilities in this new relationship.

> *I was nauseous and tingly all over.*
> *I was either in love or I had smallpox.*
> —Woody Allen

This is how list maker Julie describes her first meeting with a quality prospect: "My early adventures with love relationships were full of fear, trying to get people to be right yet being careful, and never finding anyone I could last with. It was like fighting my way uphill against a rushing stream. And then I met Eric. He was the first person I had decided to go out with since making my list and he had tons of things I wanted. It was a totally amazing experience! With him, it felt like we were both walking side-by-side downstream. Everything was so comfortable and easy and it just flowed naturally. My initial impressions were confirmed the more I got to know him. It was just awesome from the very first minute!"

After the excitement of meeting a person with a lot of what you want dies down, the remaining challenge is to decide if she or he has *enough* of the things you really need to fully give yourself to the relationship. I call it "Getting Enough Right," and this is where your list making is really going to pay off.

Getting Enough Right:

*Knowing what to do
in this confusing situation
is where preparation and judgment
meet instinct and chemistry.*
—Earl Hipp

Far away there in the sunshine
are my highest aspirations.
I may not reach them,
but I can look up and see their beauty,
believe in them,
and try to follow where they lead.
—Louisa May Alcott

Getting Enough Right

Having done the life partner list work to get this far means you have an excellent chance of meeting a high-quality prospect. You're literally programmed for it. Yet even the best life partner candidates will fall a little short of the perfect person your list describes. Few list makers find someone who has 100 percent of their list attributes. In addition, while your prospect may have a lot of what you're looking for in a partner, you're going to have to decide if this person has *enough* of the important attributes to continue moving forward. Knowing what to do in this confusing situation is where preparation and judgment meet instinct and chemistry.

If you're going to have any hope of ever finding a life partner with enough right, you're going to have to master two critical skills: saying "no" and avoiding perfectionism.

Saying "No"
No matter what approach you take, you're going to have to sort through a lot of people who clearly don't meet enough of your criteria. That means unless you're dating for fun, practice, or some other reason, you'll need to learn to be very assertive and to quickly say "no thanks" to the people who aren't a fit with your list. Relationship adventures with a person who isn't "the one" will only drain away very valuable time and relationship-seeking energy. You'll get emotionally exhausted, bored, and worst of all, lose hope of ever finding the right relationship partner.

Accumulated hopelessness is the biggest challenge facing single people today. If it's time in your life to settle in with the right life partner, you have to say "no" to impulse and hold out for the person you know will work for you in the long run. That person *is* out there.

Jeannine describes this kind of challenge and demonstrates the self-discipline required to be successful in finding love on purpose:

> I had a strange dating experience where my new list really helped. I met a man who came on to me pretty strong. I was dumbfounded because this hasn't happened much in my life. He was much younger than me so I was flattered, curious, and decided to have a coffee date with him. He was extremely up-front about wanting to be friends . . . and lovers. After not dating for a long time, you can believe it was a tempting offer.

> After our date, I mentally went through my list of what I wanted and got clear he really didn't match my life partner list much at all. I responded to his next e-mail by saying I didn't think he was a good fit for what I wanted in my life. It felt sooooo good to be that clear. The clarity helped me set a solid boundary for myself and saved me a lot of time-consuming distractions.

> Someone in my Monday night prayer group said as soon as he gets clear about his intentions, the opposite shows up to see if he was serious. I think that's what happened to me, and thanks to my list, I passed the test!

By saying no to those people who don't live up to your list, even if they possess *some* very positive qualities, you're affirming you deserve the best. If you're patient and determined, you will eventually get it right.

Avoiding Perfectionism

But there is a danger in holding out for *everything* that's on your life partner list and continually saying "no." You could wait until you find a person with the "whole package". . . if you're willing to wait the rest of your life. Another word for this method is "perfectionism." Perfectionism is always looking for "what's wrong with this picture." If you have this tendency it means you never experience your life, prospective life partners, or the world around you as acceptable.

Kim has been doing some serious reflection and in an e-mail coaching exchange wondered if her expectations for a life partner were a little too high.

> I still am not convinced the man I want really exists. I demand a lot from myself and would do the same from a prospective life partner. I live a very rich and diverse life. I have a great education and I'm smart. I'm fun, athletic, adventurous, kind, generous, spiritual, and I value self-growth. Sadly, this seems to be intimidating to the men I've met.

> Can I really find all of the traits on my list in one man? Maybe deep down I'm so afraid of another false start that I've created an impossible list for anyone to fulfill. Emotionally I am more aware of my needs and, more importantly, owning my inner strength. Perhaps my lesson is to go for what I want, keep my standards high, and then trust my list, friends, and therapist to help me when someone a little less than perfect appears.

When the prospective life partners you meet are never quite good enough, you may be suffering from perfectionism. If so, you're setting yourself up for a life of disappointment. If this sounds like you, you may want to get some help learning how to let go of perfectionism and practice acceptance. Let's be clear here. I'm talking about "practicing acceptance" *after* you have checked your lists and confirmed your person has a lot of the important things you want, checked your list of deal breakers to be sure you're being true to yourself, and then gotten objectivity from someone you trust.

A number of list makers report a terribly subtle version of perfectionism. It's when you meet people with a lot right, but there's never any "chemistry." In this situation, it's not the time to practice acceptance, but to resolve the question of why people who you know would be good for you don't light your fire. Both of these forms of perfectionism are beyond the scope of this book. But they represent opportunities to start learning more about yourself with the help of a trusted professional.

The person who has many, but not all, of your "Absolutely Required" list attributes presents you with an opportunity to decide how negotiable you're going to be. Because no one will have it all, if you're ever going to be in a long-term relationship you'll have to accept a person who is less than perfect. That's when you'll need to practice acceptance.

> *The way I see it, if you want the rainbow,*
> *you gotta put up with the rain.*
> —Dolly Parton

With a high-quality list and supportive friends, you've done everything you can do to reduce your risks. Because you've done your homework, you're now as prepared as you can be for this relationship "grey area."

When a prospect comes along with many of your "Absolutely Required" and other list items and none of the deal breakers . . . if you've gotten the blessing of objective friends, and feel the chemistry is right . . . then it's time to fully open yourself to the experience. From that point on, the worst-case scenario is you might lose a little time and come up with some new attributes for your life partner list. The best-case scenario is that you will have found love, on purpose, and be able to put your life partner list away . . . possibly forever.

The best-case scenario
is that you will have found love,
on purpose,
and be able to put
your life partner list away . . .
possibly forever.
—Earl Hipp

Real love stories never have endings.
—Richard Bach

Congratulations and a Wish

You are to be congratulated for caring enough about yourself to have gotten this far. You now hold the key to your heart's desire. Anything you do as a result of reading this book will bring you closer to finding the love of your life. Even if you've only read the book, you're still better off than you were before you started. So, I congratulate you for caring enough about yourself and your life for doing something to find love on purpose.

My wish for you is that you'll find the wonderful life partner you want and deserve. In fact it's the reason I wrote this book. Because I now have an investment in your life, I want to know what happens. If you're willing, as your adventure unfolds, please share it with me by sending an e-mail to:

Stories@FindingLoveOnPurpose.com

Until the happy day when you find love on purpose, keep working at it . . . please. ***You are worth it!***

If I keep a green bough in my heart,
then the singing bird will come.
—Chinese proverb

Finding Love On Purpose Support Services

If you're having any difficulty with the steps in this book, go to the "Singles Support Services" section of the *Finding Love On Purpose* website: http://www.FindingLoveOnPurpose.com. There you'll learn about e-mail list coaching, on-line classes, and on-line support for people who are working on life partner lists. You'll also find links to websites, and recommended books for singles.

To order additional copies of this book, in print or digital format, for the single people in your life, go to the *Finding Love On Purpose* website: http://www.FindingLoveOnPurpose.com.

You can also order the book through on-line booksellers and through your local bookstore by asking for it by name.

To inquire about having Earl Hipp speak to your group or meeting, send an e-mail to:

author@FindingLoveOnPurpose.com

To read other books by Earl Hipp written for adolescents, look for these titles at your on-line or local bookseller.

♦ *Fighting Invisible Tigers: A Stress Management Guide for Teens.*

♦ *Help for the Hard Times: Getting through Loss*

♦ *Understanding the Human Volcano: What Teens Can Do about Violence*

♦ *Feed Your Head: Some Excellent Stuff on Being Yourself*

THE LISTS
Life Partner List Examples

In the section that follows you'll find the life partner lists that have been referred to in the earlier chapters of the book.

Love is the best medicine,
and there is more than enough to go around
once you open your heart.
—Julie Marie

Anne's Basic List

- He is funny, fun, and charming.
- He likes to play a lot, and "plays fair."
- He is smart, clever.
- He is kind, kind, kind.
- He sees people in a good light.
- He is a peacemaker.
- He is fit, energetic, active, and adventurous—lives a moderately healthy lifestyle.
- He is a hard worker and generous contributor.
- He is comfortable in his own skin.
- His personal growth, and that of others, is important to him.
- He respects himself.
- He is respected and sought out by colleagues, friends, and family.
- He is noted for his integrity.
- He is open to ideas and to others.
- He is happy and challenged in his career or taking steps to make changes—now.
- He laughs at himself.
- He'll think I am funny, smart, clever, and enormously attractive.
- He needs to be at least as tall as me (5' 9").
- He has his own children; he loves them and relates to them well.
- He is flexible.
- He is socially savvy.
- He has read or at least is familiar with the book *Passages*.
- He dances.

Anne's Basic List
(Continued)

- He is tidy in some areas of his life but not all.
- His personal hygiene is important to him.
- He has a high boiling point.
- He is awake and aware of what is going on around him.
- He has a spiritual life.
- He is a good listener.
- He reads a lot.
- He is available.
- He is attractive.
- He is respectful.
- He is a good lay, and loves to give and receive snuggles.

*I came here tonight because when you realize you want
to spend the rest of your life with somebody, you want
the rest of your life to start as soon as possible.*
—Billy Crystal
From the movie *When Harry Met Sally*

Anne's First Sorted List

Absolutely Required Attributes

- He is funny, fun, and charming.
- He likes to play and "plays fair."
- He is smart, clever.
- He is kind, kind, kind.
- He sees people in a good light.
- He is fit, energetic, and active—lives a moderately healthy lifestyle.
- He is a hard worker and generous contributor.
- He has a healthy financial life, has retirement secure, and has money to play with.
- He is comfy in his own skin.
- His personal growth, and that of others, is important to him.
- He respects himself.
- He is respected and sought out by colleagues, friends, and family.
- He is noted for his integrity.
- He is open to ideas and to others.
- He is patient with people.
- He is tolerant.
- He is happy and challenged in his career or taking steps to make changes—now.
- He laughs at himself.
- He'll think I am funny, smart, clever and enormously attractive.
- He needs to be at least as tall as me (5' 9").

Anne's First Sorted List
(Continued)

- He has older than teenage children, loves them, and relates to them well.
- He is flexible.
- He is socially savvy.
- He has read or at least is familiar with the book *Passages*.
- He doesn't let dogs lick his face.
- His personal hygiene is important to him.
- He has a high boiling point.
- He is awake and aware of what is going on around him.
- He has a spiritual life and will share that with me, even go to church with me.
- He is a good listener.
- He is thoughtful.
- He is a good lay, and loves to give and receive snuggles.
- He lives no more than ½ hour from me.
- He fits into my life.
- He is available.
- He is attractive.
- He is respectful.
- He likes to travel and play with me—we will go to Ireland, Italy, and France, and visit small towns as well as big cities.
- He can keep up with me physically, and likes to ride, roller-blade, and hike.
- He likes to cook and entertain.
- He has good friendships of his own.

Anne's First Sorted List
(Continued)

<u>Important Attributes</u>

- He is between forty-five and sixty years old.
- He is tidy in some areas of his life but not all.
- He reads a lot.
- He is a peacemaker.

<u>Nice to Have Attributes</u>

- He dances.

Sex without love
is an empty gesture.
But as empty gestures go,
it is one of the best.
—Woody Allen

Anne's Second Sorted List

Absolutely Required Attributes

- He is funny, fun, and charming.
- He likes to play and "plays fair."
- He is smart, clever.
- He sees people in a good light.
- He is fit, energetic, and active—lives a moderately healthy lifestyle.
- He is a hard worker and generous contributor.
- He has a healthy financial life, has his retirement secure, and has money to play with.
- He is comfy in his own skin.
- His personal growth, and that of others, is important to him.
- He respects himself.
- He is respected and sought out by colleagues, friends, and family.
- He is noted for his integrity.
- He is open to ideas and to others.
- He is patient with people.
- He is tolerant.
- He is happy and challenged in his career or taking steps to make changes—now.
- He laughs at himself.
- He'll think I am funny, smart, clever, and enormously attractive.
- He needs to be at least as tall as me (5' 9").
- He has had children: he loves children and relates to them well.

Anne's Second Sorted List
(Continued)

- He is flexible.
- He is socially savvy.
- He doesn't let dogs lick his face.
- His personal hygiene is important to him.
- He has a high boiling point.
- He is awake and aware of what is going on around him.
- He has a spiritual life.
- He is a good listener.
- He is thoughtful.
- He is a good lay, and loves to give and receive snuggles.
- He fits into my life.
- He is available.
- He is attractive.
- He is respectful.
- He likes to travel and play with me.
- He can keep up with me physically.
- He has good friendships of his own.

Important Attributes

- He is between forty-five and sixty years old.
- He lives no more than ½ hour from me.
- He dances.
- He has read or at least is familiar with the book *Passages*.
- He is a peacemaker.
- He will go with me to Ireland, Italy, and France—we'll visit small towns as well as big cities.

Anne's Second Sorted List
(Continued)

<u>Nice to Have Attributes</u>

- He will go to church with me.
- He is tidy in some areas of his life but not all.
- He reads a lot.
- He likes to ride, rollerblade, and hike.
- He likes to cook and entertain.

*We don't believe in rheumatism
and true love until after the first attack.*
—Marie E. Eschenbach

Anne's Sorted and Prioritized List

<u>Absolutely Required Attributes</u>

- He is kind, kind, kind.
- He is available.
- He is tolerant.
- He is comfy in his own skin.
- He is a good listener.
- He is funny, fun, and charming.
- He is thoughtful.
- He is smart, clever.
- He respects himself.
- He laughs at himself.
- He is a good lay, and loves to give and receive snuggles.
- He is noted for his integrity.
- He is open to ideas and to others.
- He'll think I am funny, smart, clever, and enormously attractive.
- He is respectful.
- He is fit, energetic, and active—lives a moderately healthy lifestyle.
- His personal growth, and that of others, is important to him.
- He can keep up with me physically.
- He is respected and sought out by colleagues, friends, and family.
- He needs to be at least as tall as me (5' 9").
- He is happy and challenged in his career or taking steps to make changes—now.

Anne's Sorted and Prioritized List
(Continued)

- He has had children: he loves children; and relates to them well.
- He is flexible.
- He is socially savvy.
- His personal hygiene is important to him.
- He fits into my life.
- He has a high boiling point.
- He is awake and aware of what is going on around him.
- He is patient with people.
- He has good friendships of his own.
- He doesn't let dogs lick his face.
- He sees people in a good light.
- He is a hard worker and generous contributor.
- He has a healthy financial life, has his retirement secure, and has money to play with.
- He likes to play and "plays fair."
- He is attractive.
- He has a spiritual life.
- He likes to travel and play with me.

Important Attributes

- He is between forty-five and sixty years old.
- He lives no more than ½ hour from me.
- He dances.
- He has read or at least is familiar with the book *Passages*.
- He is a peacemaker.

Anne's Sorted and Prioritized List
(Continued)

- He will go with me to Ireland, Italy, and France—we'll visit small towns as well as big cities.

<u>Nice to Have Attributes</u>

- He will go to church with me.
- He is tidy in some areas of his life but not all.
- He reads a lot.
- He likes to ride, rollerblade, and hike.
- He likes to cook and entertain.

Each of us at any time and space is doing the very best we can with what we have.
—Louise L. Hay

Bill's Sorted and Prioritized List

SHE *MUST* HAVE the following characteristics:

- She is open and honest.
- She must truly mean what she says and not just say what she thinks I want to hear . . . too many arguments that way.
- She is healthy . . . she won't be in the early stages of a long-term illness, with all the caretaking and the wear and tear on people that it can lead to.
- She is a Catholic woman over 65.
- She is average build and my height . . . it's just more comfortable, appealing, and physically pleasing if we fit together and she looks good to me.
- She is open to spending time together.
- She is a nonsmoker.
- She is fair and reasonable when there are disagreements.
- She enjoys travel and sightseeing.
- She is a good listener.
- She is sensual, enjoys touching and sex.
- She is social, has her own opinions, friends, and interests. She's not dependent on me socially.
- She enjoys reading and occasional TV.
- She enjoys classical music and some opera.
- She likes dogs.

Bill's Sorted and Prioritized List
(Continued)

<u>**SHE *MAY* HAVE**</u> the following characteristics:

- She may be open to a relationship with my kids and grandkids, and I would do the same.
- She may attend church more than once a week.
- She may want to live in a clean home.
- She may be a good cook; if not, we'll have to figure out how we're going to eat together because of my dietary needs.
- She may want to live in Arizona at least part of the year.
- She may enjoy social drinking.

One is never too old to yearn.
—Italian Proverb

Anne's Detailed List

<u>Absolutely Required Attributes</u>

- He is kind, kind, kind—he is compassionate and has a big heart.
- He is available—I won't date a married man unless he is divorced and has lived away from his wife for quite awhile.
- He is tolerant—patient with people.
- He is comfy in his own skin—he is secure with who he is… doesn't try too hard around others…is ok with himself.
- He is a good listener—pays attention to me and draws me out.
- He is funny, fun, and charming—he makes me laugh, has a sophisticated sense of humor, a quick wit, we have good banter; he is playful, lighthearted, and engaging.
- He is thoughtful—thinks before he acts/speaks.
- He is smart and clever—he is intelligent, well read, aware, creative, and bright.
- He respects himself—doesn't put himself down.
- He laughs at himself—accepts his shortcomings and is capable of self-deprecating humor.
- He is a good lay, and loves to give and receive snuggles—I mean it. Good lover.
- He is noted for his integrity—he is known for his honesty.
- He is open to ideas and to others—has an open mind.
- He'll think I am funny, smart, clever, and enormously attractive—he worships the ground I walk on.
- He is respectful—he is considerate.

Anne's Detailed List
(Continued)

- He is fit, energetic, and active—lives a moderately healthy lifestyle. he engages in physical activity and regularly participates in sports.

- His personal growth and that of others is important to him— he is committed to learning new things, is willing to look at what isn't working in his personal life. He is interested in continuing self-discovery, is comfortable making mistakes, and expects the same from me.

- He can keep up with me physically—isn't a slouch.

- He is sought out by colleagues, friends, and family—he is respected by others.

- He needs to be at least as tall as me (5' 9").

- He is happy and challenged in his career or taking steps to make changes, now—I expect to be connected to a winner career-wise. Someone who MAKES his career happen.

- He has had children; he loves children and relates to them well—as in understands them, is engaged with them, appreciates them, strives to see things from their perspective and remembers what it's like to be their age.

- He is flexible—can change plans when stuff comes up.

- He is socially savvy—knows what to say, can read people— knows when to listen, knows when he is going too far, is not ingratiating.

- His personal hygiene is important to him—showers regularly, isn't stinky—is very clean.

- He fits into my life—I don't have to change my life for him— fits with my friends and family.

Anne's Detailed List
(Continued)

- He has a high boiling point—tolerant and not quick to anger.
- He is awake and conscious of what is going on around him.
- He is patient with people.
- He has good friendships of his own—does not rely on me for his friendships. He is resourceful enough to find his own people.
- He doesn't let dogs lick his face—I hate dog germs on faces. UGH!
- He sees people in a good light—has a positive outlook and is forgiving of people's shortcomings, tolerant.
- He is a hard worker and generous contributor—he is diligent in his work and gives to the world.
- He has a healthy financial life, has his retirement secure, and has money for play.
- He likes to play and "plays fair"—he can be goofy, not stiff, he doesn't take advantage of people, and he's not mean.
- He is attractive—he attracts people.
- He has a spiritual life—is open for discussion as to our different beliefs, but it would be nice to have someone who worships with me and prays.
- He likes to travel and play with me—he will be my travel companion, has a lust for travel, will make travel together a joy.

<u>Important Attributes</u>

- He is between forty-five and sixty years old
- He lives no more than ½ hour from me—our relationship won't be a big commuting effort.

Anne's Detailed List
(Continued)

- He dances—okay, he is GREAT at dancing.
- He has read or at least is familiar with *Passages*—is interested in women, learns about women.
- He is a peacemaker—here we are at compassionate again. He gives himself…to the world.
- He will go with me to Ireland, Italy, and France—we'll visit small towns as well as big cities.

<u>Nice to Have Attributes</u>

- He will go to church with me.
- He is tidy in some areas of his life but not all—I don't want to live with a perfectionist, but don't want a slob either.
- He reads a lot—books of all kinds, reads the paper, news magazines.
- He likes to ride, rollerblade, and hike.
- He likes to cook and entertain.

Printed in the United States
201776BV00011B/158/A